PRACTICING THE WORLD

PRACTICING THE WORLD

JUDITH SORNBERGER

CavanKerry Press LTD.

CavanKerry Press Ltd.
Fort Lee, New Jersey
www.cavankerrypress.org

Publisher's Cataloging-In-Publication Data
(Prepared by The Donohue Group, Inc.)
Names: Sornberger, Judith.
Title: Practicing the world / Judith Sornberger.
Description: First edition. | Fort Lee, New Jersey : CavanKerry Press Ltd., 2018.
Identifiers: ISBN 9781933880693
Subjects: LCSH: Sornberger, Judith—Poetry. | Grief—Poetry. | Nature—Poetry. | Spouses—Poetry. | Cancer—Poetry. | Spirituality—Poetry.
Classification: LCC PS3569.O6765 P73 2018 | DDC 811/.6—dc23

Cover photograph by Yolfie
Cover and interior text design by Ryan Scheife, Mayfly Design
First Edition 2018, Printed in the United States of America

LaurelBooks
CavanKerry Press

Practicing the World is the 12th title of CavanKerry's Literature of Illness imprint.
LaurelBooks are fine collections of poetry and prose that explore the many poignant issues associated with confronting serious physical and/or psychological illness.

CavanKerry Press is grateful for the support it receives from the New Jersey State Council on the Arts.

ALSO BY JUDITH SORNBERGER

POETRY

Wal-Mart Orchid (2011)
Bones of Light (2003)
Bifocals Barbie: A Midlife Pantheon (1996)
Judith Beheading Holofernes (1993)
Open Heart (1993)

MEMOIR

The Accidental Pilgrim: Finding God and His Mother in Tuscany (2015)

In memoriam

Bruce Brian Barton

1953–2012

CONTENTS

I

II

III

PRACTICING THE WORLD

I

HAPPY HOUR

Ever since the first snow
following your death
deer have been appearing
in our yard around the time
we'd return to the fire
to drink martinis.

When the first pair emerged
in their dusky coats, one gazed
so long into my eyes
I almost believed I'd entered
the dream I've been craving—
the one where you return
in a disguise I see right through.

In our early days I said you seemed deer-like
with your fawn-dark eyes, delicate wrists.
What about my studly biceps?
you asked, flexing. Each night I enter sleep,
ears perked for your laughter
or for the soft crush of hooves on snow.

I drift back to the earliest days
of deer and human,
through hunger and wonder,
to the magic of sudden apparition
under the opal moon's hypnosis.
Back to the ancient belief
that a deer's luminous leap
could leave this world
and land in the next.

This afternoon when I found an antler
in the snow-dazed garden
I didn't recognize it.
Rib-length, it was pronged
the way I pictured your bones
when pain pierced you from within.

But as my fingers closed
over its cool curve,
all the heat of the buck stung my eyes.
His loss is temporary.
His new antlers will bud
in time for mating season.
And I will be watching.

THE CONNAGH

One morning in County Kildare
long before you were ill
I was watching the new sun brush
the meadow's lush coat
when a copper mare and her foal
sprinted in tandem across it,
the child a bright shadow
of its mother, their muscles
glistening like joy, as if
the two were reunited after
a lifetime in separate pastures.

I almost couldn't bear such beauty
without you, waiting at home
for my return. Even snapping photos,
I knew they'd never show
my heart racing alongside.

Any more than I could know
what you felt these last weeks—
legs giving out beneath you,
a thousand needles in the slightest motion.
Or how it felt to shed your weary body.

Some say there is a tunnel and a white light,
a loving being who takes your hand.
But here's the afterlife I'd give you:
you slide through darkness
into a body fresh as sunrise,
rise on legs that wobble
only for a moment. Then
the dancing over timeless pastures
flank to flank with your creator.

SILENT NIGHT

Every carol this December
sings your silence.
I drive the icy roads
we used to sing on
to distract ourselves from danger,
taking turns choosing the tunes
till we ran out of verses.

Or until your reedy voice cracked
on a high note (or emotion) and,
embarrassed, you'd start replacing
sacred words with naughty ones.
It came upon a midnight clear,
I'd begin, and you'd follow,
that glorious dong of old.

Or you'd start, *Angels we have*
heard when high, and I'd refuse
to go on till you promised
to sing straight. But during
"The First Noel" you'd wander
off again, a wayward lamb,
to certain poor shepherds
who *lay humping their sheep*.

You are going straight to hell,
I'd giggle. You never stopped,
even when our headlights
illuminated storms of swirling stars
and I begged you to pull over.
Maybe you knew
you wouldn't die that way.

Alone on a cold winter's night,
swaddled in the whispering
heat of our all-wheel-drive,
I'm no longer terrified

of icy roads. In fact, I'm almost
hoping that one of these nights
I'll spin off in your direction,
singing *Sle-ep in heavenly piss.*

STEPPING OUT

Even in the early morning
of my widowhood, I'd wake
and step outside the house
to thank the light for life,
even though flesh was the trap
I'd writhed and wailed within
throughout the night.

Even this morning that echoes
the April one I'd delayed
leaving your arms,
and you wrote:
Don't worry.
When you return
I will be here.

Even after this winter's long torture
when spring seems too easy—
a happy ending stuck on by a simpleton,
a psalm of praise denying
the moaning ones before it,
the teeth grinding to come.

I let myself be lulled
to sleep by peepers,
cock my head come morning
for the raucous ring of red-winged
blackbirds opening the day.

As always, the early air
is revelation, and my face
turns upward like a leaf
that can't resist the sun.

Do I betray you when I shed
sorrow's thick coat,
itching to join coyotes

gathering at twilight
on the hill behind our home?

Or is yours one of the howls
that marry pain and celebration?
Either way, I must bless
each touch on my cheek—
each raindrop, sunray, snowflake.

GRIEVANCE

Why aren't you here to bury your nose
in the dusty perfume of Brigit's brindle fur,
to let the rose petal of her tongue loose
on your cheek, to scratch the white patch
beneath her chin and hear her soft snorts
of deep pleasure, to love perfectly
this one creature?

Since you died, I take her out at night,
and she promptly squats to pee, then wanders
the snow-crusted yard to snack on deer scat.
No matter how long I shiver in the dark, pleading—
as I'd pled with God for your life under those stars—
she will not poop.

Before bed I discover the cluster of turds
left in one of her new secret spots.
Once I'd have barked *naughty girl.*
But hell, I half-envy her eloquence.
I clean it up and lift her to the bed
where she used to stretch between us.

Now she seeks the side
where your warmth was.
But sometime in the night
she must give up,
briefly forgive me,
for I wake with her spine
pressed into mine.

ANNUNCIATION, THE ROCKIES

House sparrow, I thought
as she meandered toward me
down the trail through easing rain—
a tiny woman, hair a hazy gray.
I'd wanted to be startled
by the showy gold and scarlet
of the western tanager or at least
the stormy blue of Steller's jay
and almost passed her by, but
Are you here for the Bolder Boulder?
she asked, cocking her head
as if assessing what I was made of,
announcing her plan to walk
the 5K at 73 for the first time.

Thirty years her junior,
I had no such intention,
and before my eyes she changed
into another species—
purple facets dangling
from her earlobe—amethyst,
my birthstone. *Mine, too,*
she grinned. *From my husband,*
God rest him, and she reached
up to touch one.

After he died, she'd sold all
but car, clothes, and the jewelry
he gave her—all that fit
this new, portable life.
Rain lifted, dragonflies swooped in,
swirled a sapphire halo.
She extended her hand, and damned
if one didn't land on her finger
right beside the opal teardrop.

Does anyone truly think
her mate will die?
Yet twenty years after
that morning on the mountain,
mine does, and for months I trudge
from one drab day into another.
Until this morning when she
flits across my memory with
all the sparkle of the sun
lighting on each jewel,
as though she'd flown across
unimaginable distances
to say, *Fear not*,
almost making me believe
that one day this long molting
will be over and I'll emerge
a member of her species.

FLIRTING WITH DOGS

When you're a widow you get
your kicks where you can.
Hey cutie! you call to the blond
cocker spaniel hanging out
the window in the car beside you.
Male or female—who cares?

Your husband used to cringe
when you'd bend down to kiss
a strange mutt on the snout.
Good way to get your face torn off,
he'd warn. But now you smooch
whatever pooch you please—

the eager Shih Tzu, the shy greyhound,
the bad boy boxer who slipped
his collar and went AWOL—
all races, all creeds, even
dogs with no breeding whatever.

You don't vow to love them forever,
believe you can keep them from harm.
You don't worry whether one strays,
is tough to train, leaves a coat of hair
on the sofa or slobbers when excited.

All you want is a chance
to kneel in the grass
and look into their eyes—
for one moment to connect
to one another. You know
that's all you can ask for.

YOU COULDN'T BELIEVE AS I DID

What became of the nice pagan girl
I married? you complained
one morning after I'd found my way
to the church down the street
and kept walking back every Sabbath.

Over dinner you'd quiz me
on the sermon, argue with the absent preacher,
and me if I defended *his BS.*
Maybe you resented any other guy—
him or Christ—having any say in my life.

Still, each Christmas you'd present me with a cross—
one Celtic, one amethyst and gold, one silver filigree—
to kiss the hollow at the base of my throat,
even as you reiterated your position:
You were good with God, no question.
It was the Jesus piece you couldn't swallow.

When I left that church, you seemed sad,
as though our spirited debates had been
a welcome catechism, as though I'd worn
and carried with me the facet of you
that craved a faith that could be sung
in hymns of childhood without choking.

When cancer rose up the chain
of your spine, you shocked me,
suggesting we find *a spiritual structure*
for the time ahead—time we believed
might yet be months or years.
How about a visit, I suggested, from the local priest
who'd had dinners delivered to our door?

When you agreed, I should have figured
you were up to something—something
I wasn't onto until long after

her visits and your passing,
when I was kneeling in her congregation,
adorned by your last cross—the one
studded in amber—leaning into
the sly warmth of your intention.

BENEATH THE SUGAR MAPLE, LATE OCTOBER

As each crimson leaf
becomes one corpuscle
of a dervish's
               brief body
twirling in the blue
   breeze of morning,
I remember what lives
in me besides your death,
the trance of loss
dropping for one moment
beneath the tree's bright
       ecstasy of bleeding.

ALL HALLOWS' EVE

I wish you could hear your stepson
recalling how you'd transform him
into whatever he wanted to be
at this time of ghosts and glamours.
At eight, he asked you to make
him a werewolf. You sat him
on a kitchen chair and knelt to dab
on the smoke-brown makeup.
He closed his eyes so you could
touch even his eyelids—short,
tender strokes—like a father
who'd always loved him.

He can still smell the spirit
gum, pungent with mystery,
for affixing fur to his cheeks.
When you raised the hand mirror
like a startled "O" to his vision,
he stared at the creature he'd become—
one to outroar the dad in his dreams—
the so-called *real* dad—
whose yellow eyes snarled
from a lion's face.

As if he carried your genes,
he too started losing his hair
at eighteen. You tried to teach
him the art of your combover
to disguise the bald spot,
but most days he dons a blond
ponytail wig. Nearly forty, he wears
makeup, too—mascara and eyeliner.
Fuck the rednecks in the Wal-Mart
parking lot who yell *Faggot!*
He doesn't have to let rage turn him
into someone he doesn't like.
He says you showed him
he could be whoever he wanted.

THE WIDOW'S DOLL

My love gave me a baby
at Christmastime last year.
Sculpted by an artist,
her cheeks were even smoother
than my long-ago young's were,
and briefly I stroked them.
But his stubbled cheeks
I could have touched forever.

This year my friend sends
me a grown-up doll
gouged from soft wood—
her skin a map of scars,
hair a forlorn black pelt,
gaping mouth more wound
than facial feature.

Does she mean for me
to read myself
in the bulging eyeballs,
the lightless irises
painted off-center?

As a girl I half believed
my dolls arose at midnight
to play school and have
tea parties without me,
but I couldn't stay awake
long enough to learn the truth.

This doll is not allowed
to close her eyes.
She must witness
me leaving our bed
to wander late night hallways
howling. How to believe
her maker ever loved her?

ECHO, LATE WINTER

on a line from a rabbi's prayer in a Hasidic tale

Lord, let this world continue one more day
if you must as grief gnaws at our bones
and snow drifts over us in endless waves.

In one way or another we're all strays.
Let starving dogs have one more night to roam.
Lord, let this world continue one more day.

Perhaps a day for sniffing at the graves
where lie our abandoned prayers and poems
buried by the snow in endless waves.

A day of pawing through what can't be saved,
to lose claws digging to an ancient home.
Lord, let this world continue one more day.

Let us create a keening in our cave,
cry for every creature we have known
buried by the snow in endless waves.

Let our warm hands give shape to frozen clay—
a beautiful container for our moans.
Lord, let this world continue one more day
as snow drifts over us in endless waves.

LAPLAND DANCE

My first dance after my mate died
comes in the dark cave of a bar
well inside the Arctic Circle.
Returning from a reindeer ride
and stories round the fire in a *lavvu*
about the firefox whose tail swirled
the aurora borealis through the night,
our bus takes a break from the blur
of driving snow and darkness.

I'm sipping a cloudberry and vodka
when this local—not bad-looking—
stumbles into me. No words,
just grabs my arm and gestures
toward the dance floor. The wall behind
the band gleams cherry and lime—
a glass version of the Northern Lights
I won't see for the cloud cover.

So what the hell, I figure, letting him
lead me into music more familiar
than it should be—*Goodbye Joe,*
me gotta go, me-oh, my-oh,
cause tonight I'm gonna meet
my cara mio—a tune I'd danced to
long before I met my husband.
Son of a gun, gonna have big fun
on the bayou. But in Finnish,
the words can't be farther from Cajun,
sung by guys who wouldn't know
a bayou if it froze over.

Raucous as a stormy sea,
he dips and rocks us,
and I can't be more distant
from the steady arms I've lost.

Except when drunk guy
swings me and I giggle,
I hear laughter falling
from the stars.

II

MAKING LOVE

Because no one touches me now
as you did, I begin to know why
you wouldn't learn to change
the urine bag stuck to you
after your bladder was doomed.
And why you asked me to change
the dressing over the incision
that wouldn't stop weeping
though you could have done it.

I'd be washing loads of dishes,
sheets, towels, pajamas
that seemed to stack up as I slept,
and hear you call me to our bed
as you used to sometimes
when I'd risen early,
lifting the quilt to invite me
in with a speculative grin.

But now I arrived winded from stairs
with warm washcloths
to ease the release of bag and bandage,
with gauze and scissors and cream.
When you laid a hand on my thigh,
I called on tenderness to cover impatience,
my fingers searching for the tempo
to minimize stinging,
the pressure to adhere without hurting.

And now I recall how
when I glanced up
your eyes lay down in mine
as though they would
rest there forever.

RESCUED DRESS

Every girl I knew grew up
coveting this gown.
You know the one:
in the end Cinderella wore it,
Snow White and Sleeping Beauty, too.
Didn't all our stories end
with dreaming ourselves
into its silky arms?

At eighteen I fashioned
my wedding gown after the one
Olivia Hussey donned
to become Juliet.
My mother let me
have my way, although
she knew he wasn't right
for me, bought the pattern
I selected and the ivory satin,

gave them to my grandmother
who stitched me into
my destiny, trimming neckline,
wrists and bodice with pearls
as tiny as seedling tears.

As it turned out, Mom was right,
as mothers tend to be.
But how to throw out the gown
which now seemed to tell
its own story?

I couldn't keep it with me,
not after I remarried
in a dress bought off the rack.
So it went with Mom
from home to home, hiding
in basements and closets.

But now, moving to a small apartment,
she grew ruthless in her packing.
Helping her, you peeked
into one box before
hauling it to the dumpster.
And there it was: my dress.
Still in one piece, still white
despite its banishment to darkness.
You carried it to me
softly draped over one arm:
Don't you want to keep this?

How can I say no
to such a man, one
who reads the secret text
that lies like intricate lingerie
beneath such a dress?

Who understands
how a gift can survive,
even surpass, its first story,
flowing now into the tale
of his hands
making this offer.

WIDOW IN LATE MAY

Today it's all *pas de deux*
at the birdfeeder
we once watched together
from the kitchen table,
coffee mugs lifted to our lips.
First last year's cardinal couple
gliding from the wings of pine
and maple in a dazzling comeback.
Then from far beyond my vision
the garnet-hearted grosbeak
lights beside his modest bride,
sidesteps toward her, seed in beak.

It's tempting to believe
you're feeding me this vision
from somewhere beyond imagination,
somewhere that surpasses
skin and feather, time and weather.

I've never prayed to wear wings
until this morning—
wings to lift me past
even the sweetest trill,
tastiest seed of this moment.
Beyond even the memory
of our shaking a tail feather
to Motown tunes in the kitchen
while dinner simmered.
Beyond spring's ancient
serenade of yearning.

THE ROSE

I know I keep calling you back,
screaming into the black end
of every day. I know
I need to stop, to let you go.
I know.

Soothing your swollen feet
with ginger oil,
I told you to let go.
I don't know if you heard.
There was no holding you here.

And when you died, I prayed
you'd return in a dream.
Even in disguise I'd recognize you.
But recalling how you'd roll
your eyes when I'd begin our breakfasts
with *I had the weirdest dream*,
I should have known
you wouldn't choose that scene.

So how can I keep driving
this morning past the deer
lying on the shoulder, a blood
rose blooming from its anus?
I can't do a thing

but stop, kneel down, observe
the torn-off hoof, lay my palm
over the twitching skin,
and wait. It is nothing.
It is what you'd do.

HOME REPAIR

After you died I broke down and called the plumber
to end the upstairs toilet's ceaseless weeping.
Strange how a mumble morphs into a drummer.

So much had gone undone your final summer
as chemo and retching replaced housekeeping.
After you died I broke down and called the plumber.

When we first wed, if something broke, you'd fumble
through a litany of tools, curses, and bleeping.
Strange how a mumble morphs into a drummer.

But after thirty years you rarely bumbled
any task from torn screens to faucets leaking.
After you died I broke down and called the plumber.

Since the dryer wouldn't dry, though our clothes tumbled,
I ran it all day long while you were sleeping.
Strange how a mumble morphs into a drummer.

At the last you'd curse your weakness and your failure,
still laboring to curb my eyes' seeping.
After you died I broke down and called the plumber.
Strange how a mumble morphs into a drummer.

GRIEF IS NOT A DOG

you can decide not to adopt.
It will find its own way in.
You can't guard all
your chambers forever.
Once it's inside, don't even
try to put it on a schedule
of feeding, walks and all
such nonsense. Grief has
its own sloppy timing.
Feeds on your heart
when it's hungry, poops
wherever it pleases.

Grief stays up all night howling,
too bad if you can't sleep.
And when you finally nod off,
it's there, too, stalking your dreams,
sniffing out your hiding places,
laying down a soundtrack
of moans and whining.

Grief curls up on the carpet,
pretends to be sleeping.
Then, suddenly, it lunges—
knocks you to the ground
and mounts your torso,
laps up the drops of salt
it's always craving.

WARNING

A widow is a window
onto a certain abyss.
Still-coupled friends dare
a glance through my dark glasses.
Curious, of course, but cautious
not to look too long.

A widow is a billboard
on a highway that could send
you through the windshield
of conjecture. An ad for all
you don't want.

A widow is a sign
that reads *wrong way*.
Trust me—we're all
driving the wrong way.

A widow is a siren
keening to the sea.
Lulled by waves,
her hoarse lament turns sweet,
lures you into believing
that there is another life
to swim to.

A widow is a spyglass
onto a rock island
where you must die or shuffle
the DNA of what you've been
into a strange, new creature
stumbling through a clumsy
version of survival.

TWO PANES

for Bruce, who liked Edward Hopper

1. *Morning Sun*

If you've ever woken
suddenly alone
with the sun screeching
in your face,
you know this woman—
no longer young, but alive
with awful new knowledge.

She's pulled herself up
to sit on sheets
smooth as a virgin's skin,
drawn knees toward her chest
and crossed her hands
below them.

Still, the light advances
up her thigh, reddens
her cheek—brute angel
who won't let her fall
back into the shadows.

2. *Cape Cod Morning*

Hopper never gives
us a woman's eyes.
Here in this bay window
only her profile framed
by black shutters
like margins on paper
mourners used once.
Fingers gripping an end
table, she leans into light
that nearly erases

her features, converting
her into a beacon
for what will ever stay
beyond her vision.

ANSWERING MACHINE

What if it really had the answers?
Would it tell me why I taped over
your greeting after just a year—
your voice lifting each time
it spoke our names together,
sounding hopeful and jaunty
when you asked for a message
as though you were up for
whatever was left there?

Of course, you recorded it
long before your diagnosis,
before the surgery we were told
would give you many years.
When the waiting room phone rang
I leapt for it, blurting, *How'd it go?*
The surgeon's answer, though kindly
spoken, didn't encourage.

In sympathy cards, your students wrote
of your *gentle voice*, your *soothing voice*,
and I was shocked. From the start
I'd loved your poems, your wit,
your laugh, your touch, so much else.
How could I have missed adding
your voice to that long list?

In an NPR interview yesterday
Bing Crosby's widow stated
that she loved the Christmas season
since everywhere she went
she heard him singing.
I had to pull over, let my sobs
bury their voices.

Forgive me. I didn't know
I loved your voice
till it was silent.

LATE JANUARY

after a 9th-century Irish poem

I have news for you:
It's eight below here,
and last night the furnace died.
The leanest maple branches
gleam like ice picks
in morning's frigid light.
I bundle up and nudge
a suet cake into its cage,
fingers stiff as unlit tapers.
But the chickadee snips seed
from the sumac's torch.
This world doesn't need me
except maybe to report
that snow blossoms
in the white pine
are as beautiful
as any crocus.
That is my news.

STILL LIFE

Get an artist over here
to paint this image of eternity
that isn't—snow reposing
in the eastern field
as if it had no memory
of any other home.

So much a single, settled thing,
glittering beast asleep
under the stars,
who'd believe it
once was multitudes—
an exodus of crystals,
each brief life drifting
through the sky to earth?

Like your perspective
on the afterlife—
an aggregate of souls
whose edges melt and merge.
Remember how we'd argue
over our martinis
(mine gin and yours vodka)?

I insisted on the soul's integrity
and that I'd damn well
find you when I died.
Although now you know
the secrets hidden under snow,
your frozen lips aren't telling.

MONUMENT

Even though all my prayers end
in the name of Christ, Amen,
and though you are my deepest loss,
your marker, my love, bears no cross.
Accept this as my final gift—
to let you enter the abyss
wearing no shield of faith or creed
over your grass and clover tweed.
Your poems followed no metered line.
Your faith required no design.
And on your last nights as we prayed,
holding hands across the bed,
our words bled into one cascade
and all our differences were wed.

LAST MOVIE DATE

When she's done taking his pulse,
he asks the nurse if we can cuddle.
We encourage that here, she smiles,
not adding *at times like this.*
She and I push him to one edge
of the narrow bed, prop him
with pillows on his side
so I can slide in.

We're both broader than the first time
we arranged ourselves into sleep—
my back against his belly—and this bed
is narrower than any we've known.
If I stray from him one inch
I'll land on cold linoleum,
but his arm circles my middle
and I'm safe for this one moment.

Our nurse clicks on the classic
movie channel, and we doze
on and off to *Camelot*, a story
we could follow in our sleep,
while I try not to feel
my arm go dead beneath me.
How many times has he remarked
that he's Arthur, not Lancelot?
Like Guenevere, I love them both
and have found both—hero-lover
and sweet dreamer—in him.

Once I wake to Lance singing
If ever I would leave you . . . ,
so young and hale, he still believes
he'll always have a choice.
I know my love must leave me,
but this morning when I tried
to say some of the last,

most needful things, he begged,
Please, not yet.

So I wait like Guen before her burning,
straining to hear the rumbling hooves
of reprieve. Once he wakes
and pulls me closer, whispers
into my hair, *Thank you.*
For what? I ask.
Thank you for being my wife.
This line will never leave me.

III

MIDLIFE BEDTIME STORY

Now the last parent has died
and we have found our way back
to the page where two children
wander in the woods, trying
to leave a birth cord of crumbs
back to the body that baked them.
Only now we know that such a trail
must always be devoured by dark birds.

It's all here: the fantasy
that there will ever be a cottage
sweet as the mother's body,
that we might feed on it forever
without tummy ache or tooth decay,
nestled in its shelter, at least one lick
of icing between us and disaster.

Only now we see the cookstove
is never satisfied, and we must read
our future in its embers.

GHOST CAT

for our friend James York Glimm, folklorist (1942–2000)

Your sources claimed that the cat
called by as many names as God
doesn't haunt these mountains anymore.
But on the last day we saw you alive
Bruce and I were riding our bikes
through a warm green tunnel of leaves,
letting the breeze lift our gloom,
when we spotted him up ahead
hunting in the ditch, the long velvet rope
of his tale switching behind.

I quit pedaling, of course,
then scooted slowly closer.
That's no kitty cat,
Bruce warned from behind.
But I couldn't stop myself.
He was so beautiful, you see,
in his tawny stealth—
like a creature in a tale
that can't be true.
Like the phantom buck
in the yarns you collected,
the one no one could kill.

I felt like Mary Magdalene
standing open-mouthed
before the empty tomb.
Later I told everyone
I knew that he was back.
Most shook their heads:
probably a bobcat.
After all, there was no scat,
no road kill—no proof.

By the time they were through,
I was tempted to doubt my vision,
but how could I deny
the moment of his turning,
swiveling that old-gold gaze
deep into mine or the feeling
that he knew me?

THE NEW PLACE

For this five minutes I'm the one
who's joyous, floating in contentment
I should know better than to trust.
My friend calls to report the death
of her career in health care.
You've been on my mind, I lie.
Well, not lie, exactly. Her plight
hangs at the edge of my vision
like bag worms hanging on trees
at the border between the lawn
and woods of our new home. I suppose
something must be done. I hear
there is a spray that won't harm the finches,
chickadees, cardinal pair and rose-
breasted grosbeak we have found here.
Still, something must die.

But right now I'm caught up
in praising all trees, bushes,
and perennials strutting their stuff
with the glitz of Vegas showgirls—
frothy purple boas of the lilac,
bleeding heart dangling its pink
lockets like love tokens to sunlight.
Or geisha-like—quince with its first coral
perching on the branch like butterflies
on silk kimonos, miniature origami
cranes of honeysuckle—all flashing by
so fast I'm afraid I won't give
each its due in delight.

So why am I recalling
the night my brother-in-law died,
how we stayed up all night, couldn't keep
our eyes off Tina Turner on the tube—
all that life pulsing from every pore?

A friend tells me her father's in the ICU,
and I'm almost grateful Mom's labored
wheezing ended two years ago.
That I've been granted this breathing
space for taking in the over-the-top
sweetness of lilies-of-the-valley
without death's distraction—first Dad's
death, then hers, and then my in-laws'—
in such rapid succession
our eyes were never dry.

At least in this five minutes my sister's
new lung, harvested from the chest
of an eighteen-year-old boy,
swells like the green bud of the rhododendron
before exhaling its purple blossom.
And now, instead of trailing the oxygen
tank like a dying creature through her rooms,
its hissing breath intimate as her own, afraid
to go outside for what true air will do to her,
she's pushing her wheelbarrow
and planting a new border.

I know that none of this can last.
Any moment now the phone will ring
and my son will say he's been
deployed for the third time to Iraq.
And even if it doesn't, children
are dying right this minute in Darfur,
and instead of signing another
check to the Red Cross
I'm at the nursery selecting
Mom's favorite shade of geraniums
for the deck where just last week
white blossoms on the Bartlett pear
gave their rendition of a blizzard—
the end of a beginning—enchanting us
for one long breezy afternoon.

We're even novices enough
at mountain living to be charmed
by the bear who came by
when we were sleeping
and tore down the birdfeeders,
guzzling their seeds.

In her last days Mom was sure
a bear was chasing her through mountains.
We couldn't convince her there was no bear
or mountain in her part of Texas.
But though she had assured us
she had no fear of dying,
she knew terrifying when she saw it,
and was convinced that we were
either nuts or lying.

Of course, she saw what we would not:
that all this beauty—trees leafing
out in green so gold we squint to see it,
low-lying clouds of forsythia, viburnum—
is a scrim shielding our eyes
from what breathes deep in our woods,
from what is always coming.

INITIATION

The word for it—*period*—
suggested an ending,
but when I woke at twelve
and found the bright rose
that had bloomed on my white
panties overnight, I felt shy
with excitement as though
I'd received my first corsage
or secret kiss.

Boys like you got your blood
in sports or fighting.
During wrestling season,
you told me decades later,
you were always wadding
cotton up your bloody nose.
Later in bar fights you earned
the scars you wore like medals,
the ones my fingertips traced
when you first followed me to my bed.

In its last erratic visits,
my blood turned muddy
as trampled petals
in a ruined garden,
and your scars have faded
into rueful tales.

We thought we were done with blood
(*as well as the mud and the beer*,
you joked, toasting over dinner).
But one morning your urine turns
the toilet water scarlet as the Pinot Noir
we sipped the night before—
the last evening of a certain life.

WAITING FOR YOUR LAB RESULTS

I set off through morning mist
that sun seeps through like hope
or even joy, but I haven't pedaled far
before a snakeskin skitters across gravel.
I work hard, darling, to see it as a sign
of transformation, not of death and rebirth—
a fine theme in the great scheme of things.
But who needs it at the moment?

Now I swerve to miss a painted turtle
basking on the path, certainly a symbol
of long life, right? And its carapace
is all about protection. So I'm liking
what I'm seeing till I spot a lone
female merganser floating on a pond.
I fly past, refuse to contemplate
what's happened to her mate.
Yet I can't erase her rusty crest
or stop envisioning it as the ragged
flag of a country of one.

And as I hunch beneath pine boughs
I read each dewdrop
balanced on each needle
as clinging there,
praying not to fall
or lose itself
to morning.

STAGE 2, MAYBE STAGE 3

This morning, sipping coffee
on our deck, all above is blue
curling with white, but from behind
the line of pines, a grumbling
seizes our Shih Tzu from her nap,
sets her barking at what terrifies her.
As the rumbling deepens and draws nearer,
her bluster lifts her front paws
into the air, as if to say:
Lucky for you, thunder, I can't fly.

Like you last night barking
not really at me—or even
at the chemo that brings you
to your knees before the toilet
and sends pain streaking
through your bones like lightning—
but at the thunder you can't stop
from stalking toward us.

WAY STATION

Love, why must you grieve
that our parents never visited this home,
this joy, we've found?
True, death swooped down
for each father and each mother,
one by one, in rapid succession
like the chickadee, then the grosbeak
then the bully-boy blue jay,
landing on our feeder that perches
between lawn and mountain wildness.

Why couldn't they have lived? you ask,
to watch the birds, raccoons, and deer
from our back deck where worlds meet
and mingle at woods' edge
and red squirrels regularly crash the party.
Look at that one leaping on the tray,
chattering its scorn as it scatters
doves paused there.

Imagine how pissed off your mom would be.
Shit-asses! she'd shriek, tearing off her sandal,
aiming at one like she used to do in her backyard.
Can't you hear your father's throaty chuckle,
like the gurgle of the small stream
in our backyard after rainfall?

And, when she misses, his voice raucous
as the red-winged blackbird's,
daring her to try the other one.
Then her shrill command that he climb up
and fetch it, which he does.
Still, when he returns, offering the shoe
with a mock flourish, she swats him with it.
Always such silly squabbles were their love calls.

And can't you see my mother lounging
on a chaise, waving her cigarette as she talks,
her smoke pluming toward heaven—
high priestess of the patio?
She, who even in Omaha suburbs,
warned her daughters to beware of bears,
hopes, we know, that one will drop by.
Which reminds Dad of the time
my little sister said she was so strong
she could beat up a bear. *Hello, zoo?*
my father says, holding the phone
to his ear, as he did that day.
Say, this is Bill Mickel over on 86th Street.
Could you please send over
your biggest, meanest bear?
Can the creatures nearby tell
our laughter from our crying?

I suppose it must sound funny
when I greet the bright blood slash
of the cardinal each morning.
Hi Mom! I call to the bird
that always cheered her.
Do I believe she hears me?

When we call out to the dead, my love,
don't our own words proclaim they're here?

MY HUSBAND'S FIRST PUMPKIN PATCH

On what will be the last page of summer's
gold-leaf gospel, you and our friends' son Gabriel
make a pilgrimage to your pumpkin patch.
You already know how many bellies ripen,
half-hidden under leaves, but you let Gabe find
each one and add it to his tally, a junior
accountant of harvest abundance.

When our boys were his size, we grew
only what would grow them—tomatoes,
squash, broccoli, carrots—*need* and *feed*
the key words of that season's catechism.
But as we turn autumn's illuminated page,
those boys have long since snapped
loose from us, and our bellies
have rounded on time.

Now you are free to plant
just for the joy of witnessing
each bright planet plump up
in your square-foot universe,
prophet of the day you will carve
into one perfect pumpkin
God's crooked grin.

LEAVING THE CANCER CENTER, LATE OCTOBER

Later, during the drive home,
the news will hit us,
but now I steer you
slowly through the halls
to avoid each bump and corner,
each jolt of pain repeating that
cancer climbs your spine now.

Some people move so frigging slow,
I hear as another chair pulls up
to pass us. At first I think she's joking,
but her face wears the rage of a Greek mask.
Excuse me, I say, *but we've just received*
a tough diagnosis.

My son's been in treatment for ten years,
she snarls, and I make the mistake
of looking down at the swollen ghost face,
soot-ringed eyes. But thank the gods
I stop my hand from rising to her shoulder,
stop the pity words that taste like tears.

Now I know they'd only crack
her face to splinters. Right now
she must be Clytemnestra,
and I must stand in
for all that's killed
the beauty she gave birth to.

If she can just cling to her fury,
fingers clenched white
around the handles of his chair,
they can make it to their car,
escape this frigging moment.

PRAYER IN THE WEEKS BEFORE SURGERY

Instead of pressing palms
tight as I was taught,
I cup one palm
over the other—
fingertips to wrists—
before my belly.

This is how I show God
what I'm asking,
how I direct God's hands
to plunge into my husband's gut
where cancer harbors
in the sea of his bladder
gnawing at the shoreline.

This is how I show myself
God's hands—ribbed and tawny
as the shell called *lion's paw*
we found at Sanibel—hinged
over the bladder, holding in,
I hope, all harm.

This is how I teach myself
to sink into the place
beneath light and word,
where there is only
being held and holding.

THE CHEMO WAITING ROOM

Here everyone waits for the same miracle—
the conversion of poison to cure.
As in the churches of childhood,
the women cover their heads—
here in turbans, scarves or ball caps.
Except for one.

Small, pale, and alone,
in the bird kingdom she'd be a sparrow
with her brown checked capris and beige tee.
But the black straw boater with grosgrain bow
perched at an insouciant angle turns her
into a flashy kingfisher darting among tame ducks.

When I admire her hat, she touches the brim
to recall it, confesses she has several hundred,
started her vintage collection decades before
cancer found her. *And now*, she shrugs,
I get to wear them all!

Her favorites? She grins, throws open
the doors of her giant armoire:
There's the plum velvet with fishnet veil,
a cartwheel hat wreathed in tiny silk violets,
the scarlet cloche with an ostrich plume.
Oh, and the sequined cocktail tilt,
the Russian fur, the navy fascinator . . .

I believe she'd name them all if we had time,
try on each life she's imagined—
the coed being punted down the Thames;
the coquette sipping martinis with diplomats and spies;
the chanteuse crooning in a swanky club;
the flapper dancing till she drops.
But her name is called, she rises,
and the Infusion Suite doors sigh
closed behind her.

THE CANCER CENTER GARDEN

While chemo drips into my husband's wrist
as he watches *The View* (because, he insists,
nothing else is on), I go back to the garden
we always wander through before going inside,
marking each new stage of blooming:
first freckled stargazers performing backbends;
next roses perched like fat red birds on lime branches;
today the butterfly bush speaking in frothy purple tongues.

This steamy morning I'm looking for shade,
a place to sit and watch for birds to appear
at the boulder burbling water—
a manufactured miracle, I know, but one I need
to see the way the sparrow must—as mercy.
I'm still searching when a small voice chirps,
Is there something I can help you find?

Turning, I see a nun in crisp white, black and gray—
compact and chipper as a chickadee.
When I saw you here, she beams, clasping her hands
before her breast, *I said, Thanks be to God.*
Someone's enjoying it. Who'd believe
that, just by being here—the first person she's seen
all summer among the wing beats and the bee-hum—
just by doing what I love, I could become
what she has prayed for?

And who would guess
that in the shade
of her kind gaze
I'd find a garden to replace
the one his diagnosis drove us from—
a place to learn the prayers
that can be answered.

AFTER-CHEMO BLUES

No, he doesn't want even a sip
of ginger ale. Just please let him rest
and let this damn day drip

by and the fever lose its grip.
He won't say, but you're a pest
imploring him to try another sip.

And, furthermore, don't suggest a trip
outside to watch the wren building its nest.
Can't you just let this damn day drip

away, swallow all your stupid tips
for avoiding nausea's duress?
And, good God, spare him another sip

from this long night's overflowing cup,
all the weeks he has yet to ingest.
How can he fathom even the next drip?

Take away your cold packs and ice chips.
Hold back every sweet word and caress.
Know that he can't bear a single sip

of sound or kiss from your scared lips.
Rather, if you truly mean to bless,
let each long second in silence drip

like the poison poured into his wrist.
And as the sun's bald head begins to crest,
just accept he doesn't want a sip.
Go away and let this damn day drip.

THIS AUTUMN MORNING ARRAYS ITSELF

in layers of sheer mist before
the almost naked mountain
like a bride in a distant century
preparing to wed the man
she did not choose, yet wrapping
her shy skin in one layer
of silk over another,
slowly—a bird folding
in her wings after flight.
Finally adding her finest kimono—
dove gray stained
with crimson maple leaves—
and tying herself
with an obi of the same
burning apricot as the oak
wears outside my window.

Autumn is always an elegy—
even this one, after living
thirty years with the man
I choose again each morning,
waking in his arms folded
around me like a gown
that knows my body perfectly,
embracing and forgiving
every imperfection.
Then comes the moment
when I step, alone,
into the chill of late October,
the dress rehearsal for
what comes next.

SLOW DANCE WITH BROKEN SHOULDER

Cast and all, we dance our kitchen floor
though my broken wing holds us apart—
like some olden-time bundling board—
folded, as it is, over my heart.
This spring our woods turn young as we turn old,
though new birdsong still catches us off guard
as much as when feet lose their earthly hold.
Still, who'd believe I'd take a fall so hard?
But, love, let's be voracious as the creatures
after dozing away winter in their lairs
who guzzle all the good from our birdfeeders—
those pesky chipmunks, squirrels and black bears.
Let's dance with every hungry foe age sends us
until one finally dips us, drops us, ends us.

WATCHING YOU TEST YOUR BLOOD SUGAR

Some evenings I practice
the world without you.
I don't want to, but the sky
has ways of insisting
as it takes on the sly
intelligence of twilight.

I make myself imagine blue
without you—just one color,
just one hue—the deep lapis
of Mary's glass robe at Chartres,
that virgin blue so dazzling
I gasped at each turn
on the labyrinth.

I know I'll never make it
back to an unworried blue.
Even morning's cotton candy horizon
is now the sweetness in the blood
that warns you'll go before I do.
Go first like a kid off a ledge,
daring the dark water's
treacherous gleam.

I keep diving for the blue
deeper than morning glories
you plant for your grandfather,
deeper than the eyes
of the child you'll never father,
deeper than the rivers
of blood beneath our skin,
as though I might arrive
at the confluence
where we two
cannot be divided.

THEOLOGY

He is expecting my call, but I can't get a signal
in the monastery guesthouse and the rain
has not let up all day. I try the car, but no dice.
Standing in the deluge   I punch our number
and he answers in one ring. *Hi, it's me.*

Hi you.

How's it going at home? How's Brigit?
Nothing. *Can you hear me?*
Nothing. I start pacing, hoping to find a spot of grace.
Can you hear me?

I hear you.

How's Brigit?

I'm hoping . . . between storms
she'll stay out long . . . to poop.

You mean, she hasn't pooped all day?
Nothing. *Hello?*

Hello. You . . . breaking up.

I explain why the reception is so lousy,
hoping to impress him with my devotion.
We might as well say goodnight, I say,
and give up on this phone call.

You need to go?

No, but why stand here (he has yet to acknowledge
that I'm getting soaked just to hear his voice)
pouring words into the rain when you can't hear me?
Nothing. *Can you hear me?*

Just . . . word . . . and there.
I stop pacing. *Let's say goodnight then.*
Okay, I love . . .

I'm facing the chapel where, in a few moments, I'll be
listening to monks sing the lullaby that asks for
a safe journey through the night.
Will you love me beyond death? I hear myself asking.
Nothing.
Honey! Will you love me beyond death?
By now I'm nearly shouting.

I . . . you . . . first time . . . many times . . . discussed this?
I'll love . . . til death . . . the best I . . . do . . .

Well, fuck you then! I glance around,
hoping no monk's heard me.

What?

Never mind.
Rivulets of water cascade over my sandals, wash my toes.

I'd like to say I'll . . . beyond death, . . . can't believe
. . . afterlife. You know that.

Why not? I ask, as though standing in the downpour
gives me some special dispensation to revisit the issue.
As though his doubt might drown the small, slippery mound
of faith I stand on. As if this question of the afterlife
will be decided right now, goddammit, or never.
Nothing. *Why not?*

Because, if anything, . . . atoms floating . . .
at best part . . . giant consciousness or something.
No separate . . . self. You know I don't . . . in that.

Why not? But now he's broken up for good.
Nothing but static. When the bell starts ringing,
I slog through soggy grass to pray.
But I cannot help trying one more time.
If I get through I'll say *I love you*, won't request
a single thing beyond this moment.
Can you hear me?

ANNIVERSARY SESTINA

Even if we hadn't wed in May
under almost too-sweet apple blossoms,
spring's always an anniversary—
when winter white fractures
into all the colors we've forgotten
and each birdcall's an annunciation.

The urologist's mumbled annunciation
came to you three years ago this May.
Still our cherry tree wore party pink and we almost forgot—
celebrating thirty years—the cancer blossoming
along the boughs of old rib fractures
as we climbed waterfalls on our anniversary.

No one predicted that that anniversary
would be our last. The surgeon's annunciation
that cancer filled your trunk didn't fracture
every hope, for he offered: *You still may*
have a chance, words we gripped like blossoms
saved in pages, not to be forgotten.

If only each glad moment I've forgotten
could pop up again each year—an anniversary—
small and bold as a primrose blossom
calling out its gold annunciation,
I might live in an eternal May.
Or would that be death—the present fractured?

But one day even sorrow fractures,
which is not to say you are forgotten
or that there'll come a May
that doesn't hold these anniversaries
in balance as I hear earth's annunciation
issuing from furry tongues of iris blossoms.

This spring my new love leads me under his apple blossoms,
careful not to bump the arm I fractured

in a recent fall. The orthopedist's annunciation:
I will fully heal. I haven't forgotten
your tender care when I was in a cast one anniversary
even as another's hands dress and undress me this May.

I wish I may, we said as children when the first star blossomed,
have my wish this anniversary—that tonight's sky would fracture
with annunciation—your voice proclaiming I am not forgotten.

CODA: THREE AUTUMNS AFTER YOUR DEATH

Before the first tree goes bald
on our mountain, half the neighbors
have flown off to Florida—
the Never-Never-Land for grown-ups
where their other lives await,
hanging like brightly-patterned ghosts
in condo closets. Sometimes I envy
that existence where not a tree
in sight insists that you must die.

But if I followed, who would note
the three subspecies of red oak
outside my living room window—
one high noon yellow,
one the cerise and gold of sunset,
one the deep scarlet of a pierced heart?

I stand with them as I stood
that late November beside you—
when the leaves lay limp and tarnished
copper underneath their trunks—
beside the slim bed where you lay
in your last days, arranged
so we could watch the first snowfall—
slow, momentous, each flake perhaps
the final word on beauty.

ACKNOWLEDGMENTS

My unending gratitude and love to Bruce Barton—my late husband, writing partner, and editor.

Much love and thanks to Jill Mickel, my sister and wise mentor in widowhood, who came when we needed her and who called me every single day following Bruce's death to listen and soothe.

Many bouquets to Alison Townsend, anam cara and writing partner across the miles, and to Lilace Mellin Guignard, dear friend and nearby writing partner.

Grateful thanks to:

my writing group—Lilace Mellin Guignard, Walter Sanders, Tom Murphy, David Stinebeck, and Susan Williams Beckhorn—for their inspiration, kind suggestions, and laughter. And for deadlines!

CavanKerry Press editors Joan Cusack Handler and Teresa Carson for their belief in this collection; Starr Troup, managing editor, for her helpfulness and her patience with my Luddite tendencies; my editor Baron Wormser for his encouragement and wise suggestions.

my sons Jamie and Matthew Sornberger for their loving tributes at Bruce's funeral and their ongoing support and love.

friends whose help in the final months of Bruce's life, and following his death, I will never forget: Walter and Lynn Sanders, the Guignard family, Mary Ginn, Nancy Dart, and Tom Murphy.

Reverend Rowena Gibbons, rector of St. James Episcopal Church, whose ministry to us (even though we weren't members of her parish) was invaluable and to the congregation of St. James who welcomed me into their church and their hearts.

Karl Schneider for loving me and understanding.

The author wishes to thank the periodicals and anthology that originally published the following poems:

The Cape Rock: "Initiation," "This Autumn Morning Arrays Itself"

Image: "Prayer in the Week before Surgery," "You Couldn't Believe as I Did"

Pilgrimage: "Leaving the Cancer Center, Late October"

Poems & Plays: "Happy Hour"

Rock & Sling: "Theology"

The Untidy Season (Backwaters Press): "Way Station"

The following poems were published in *The Hard Grammar of Gratitude*, an internal chapbook appearing in *Poems & Plays* and winner of the 2010 Tennessee Chapbook Prize: "My Husband's First Pumpkin Patch," "Slow Dance with Broken Shoulder," and "The New Place.

OTHER BOOKS IN THE LAURELBOOKS SERIES

The Baby Book, Robin Silbergleid
My Crooked House, Teresa Carson
Motherhood Exaggerated, Judith Hannan
Letters From a Distant Shore, Marie Lawson Fiala
Little Boy Blue, Gray Jacobik
We Mad Climb Shaky Ladders, Pamela Spiro Wagner
Elegy for the Floater, Teresa Carson
To The Marrow, Robert Seder
Surviving Has Made Me Crazy, Mark Nepo
Body of Diminishing Motion, Joan Seliger Sidney
Life With Sam, Elizabeth Hall Hutner

This book was printed on paper from responsible sources.

Practicing the World was designed by Mayfly Design, and set in Tribute OT, created in 2003 by German type designer Frank Heine.